MARRIAGE SECOND CHANCE

By

Rev. Dr. Stephen N. Ireri

ISBN 978 – 1 – 105 – 50162 – 3

DEDICATION

This book is dedicated to my wife Mandrine W. Ireri, for her outstanding love and commitment, which she has displayed over 45 years of our living together without any quarrel as a husband and wife and as a brother and sister in Christ. She is an ideal wife and a wonderful mother to my children. She is the woman God created for me to complete me in doing what I am not able to do alone.

This is why God created male and female to become one flesh when they marry. My wife has been what I could not do. She has the missing part to complete me.

God introduced the idea of partnership with a husband and wife. This idea is not clearly understood by many people who leave God out of their marriage. Thus, through the husband and wife God continues to create and rule the world. Therefore, it is imperative that any successful marriage has to have this triune unity. God has to be involved in marriage. I have proved this to be true in our marriage. The world falls or stands when the family fabric is neglected or maintained.

Thank you my wife who is also my closest partner for your constant help and encouragement for helping me to complete my fourth book.

Special dedication goes to my dear family members namely: Sam and Mary Ireri and their children Chris, Tim and Sharon.

Silas and Mary Muthuri and their children Ken, Brian and Sam

And, last but not least, Fred and Mercy Obare and their newborn baby girl, Destiny Obare.

The unity of the family is the open door of the success which comes to any member of that family.

ACKNOWLEDEMENTS

This book has been dedicated to my beloved wife who has been the force behind its writing and who is the first to receive my acknowledgement. Her inspiration and encouragement has been enormous. Some people have supported me in many ways through the time of writing this book.

The material in this book came about by the way of revelation I got as I was thinking about the last two books I have written about marriage. As with all other books comparing with what is happening around us keep on shaping my thinking and understanding to be able to share what my research and my experiences have become something I would be proud to share with the world. I also hope that the material in this book will be a masterpiece as an illumination of the inner core forces, which broaden marriage scope to be enjoyable and successful.

Also my special thanks go to my dear and special family members who have continued to pray for the success of this book as well as with other books.

I am especially thankful to Mrs Debbie Schooley who helped in proofreading.

Additional help came from Daniel Muriithi and Fred Obare who worked tirelessly in using computer skills to shape this book.

Space would not allow me to acknowledge every body but for all others who prayed for me and encouraged me in one way or another, to them I say thank you.

CONTENTS

PREFACE

As the first reason to write this book has been explained in the introduction, so the second reason goes hand in hand with it. This book has been written to answer the cry of many married people who have come to discover that marriage

is really a good institution. To them their main finding is that if they had known in the beginning what they know now they would have done the right thing at the right time and they would have been able to avoid most of the problems they encountered.

They admit that what they have discovered is that most of the problems encountered are of their own making. Sometimes they became complacent and stopped doing those little things which did not seem so important to them but later on proved to be essential. Do not rely on teaching how to make your marriage happy**. You have what it takes to do it**. **Marriage is about giving the best service. Do better than what you do at your place of work. You are CEOs.**

What I *have heard many couples say is that* they stopped showing love thinking that they had deposited enough love so that each partner knew that he or she was loved. They failed to realize that love is like fire which needs fire wood on a daily basis so that it keeps burning. **For love to grow it must be kindled with thinking, talking and doing love is the daily routine.**

Other small things would include giving help in the house, showing appreciation for what the partner does well, telling one another how smart or beautiful he or she is, kissing whenever going out or coming in, taking time to relax on the sofas together, and many other wonderful things of which the list is endless is to be the norm. You don't need to go somewhere to pay money to be told these things. **Be serious. Be committed. Be submissive to one another and finally give love.**

Those who have been married know very well what brought them together, and what made them happy. They know whatever made each one enjoy the other, working together in the kitchen, the intimacy shared in the bedroom, sharing in helping the children with homework, and going out for walk or going out to eat**. Do these things to make your marriage last long.**

In this book I am raising the issue of looking back to your past married life see or evaluate how well you have done - whether good or bad. After prayerfully and honestly assessing the findings, then take time to look forward and decide how you are going to do things differently so that you will have a different result.

For if you continue to do the same old thing all the time you will always get the same old result. So for this reason it is necessary for you need to make some changes. I am anticipating that you will have a change both in your life and your marriage.

As you read through the sub-topic in this book, they are painting a deep and secret message for what the book offers. Mastering these sub-topics themselves will give in summary what the whole book is about. Please spend time on them and receive the understanding they offer.

Before I end this preface I would like you to focus on the factor of God as the center of the message in this book for without Him all our efforts are wasted. And the words I have borrowed from a Kikuyu Hymn Book which I have translated in English sums it all up.

"In the beginning of creation God solemnized the first marriage and blessed it. Even now He blesses Christian weddings when Christians are getting married.

O God we invite you come and give away this bride who is here, the same way you gave Eve to Adam.

And You the Holy Spirit who abides in them bless them as they kneel for your blessings.

Join their hands together – Jesus Our Savior knit their hearts together so that their love for one another may be full.

Then, be guiding and protecting them always so that their marriage relationship on earth may be enriched.

And finally, they may be able to ascend to heaven when the Lord will come for us – joining together with the Church the Bride of Christ." (From Kikuyu Hymn Book translated in English).

And to focus on the factor of God I have decided to make this book special by ending every chapter with two intriguing questions. **Try not to avoid answering my two intriguing questions: "Has God been consulted? Will God be consulted?"**

INTRODUCTION

The Reason for writing this book

This book has come to be written because of the desires of the people who read my first books. They asked whether I could give more information for those who have made a mess of their lives and are wondering whether there is any way they can salvage their marriage.

I was so surprised to know that my second book with the titled, "Marriage Without Sex," could gain readers from people who had been married over thirty or forty years. I remember when I was telling people that I was writing a book with that title, they were skeptical and some of them thought it would be a waste time to read it. Others thought it was a book for youth and all other people who did not have knowledge about marriage.

The old adage has it right that, 'never judge a book by its cover.' These reactions have kept some people away from reading the book. But it was only a matter of time. Slowly but sure, one by one some of these very people have come to me expressing the revelation they found in that book.

I remember after my book came out I took it to some pastors to announce to their congregations about my second book. When they read the title they were hesitant to announce about the new book.

Immediately I discovered they judged my book by the title. To many people the mention of sex is a taboo and to others it is a dirty thing.

So I went home, made a copy of the 'preface' of the book which gave the overall idea of what the book was about, and sent it those pastor to read. The following Sunday the pastors were able to announce the book. That action taught me two lessons.

Firstly, pastors can be a stumbling block and can hinder their congregations to know the truth. Especially these days God is revealing some wonderful truth about the Word of God.

Secondly, Many Christians have remained babies in their understanding of the Word of God because they rely on their pastors to feed them with the interpretations of what the text means. This reveals why many people have been Christians for many years yet they have remained babies, not able to read the Bible by themselves and ask the Holy Spirit to interpret the text to them.

Many people don't know that by sticking to a denomination they could loose salvation because there are some churches or denominations which teach contrary to what the Bible teaches. When these people hear the true gospel and accept it, they find that they have a problem with the pastor of that church or denomination because the truth is not what the pastor believes.

And more particularly, I am surprised to discover that the educated do not read just any book. They first check the review about the book: afterwards they are ready to read the book. I wonder why should they wait for another person to tell them what to read? Why should they be taken captives by the opinions of others?

For if the reviewer is bias he imprisons you in his way of thinking. Why don't you use your knowledge to read a book and make your personal conclusion without the influence of another?

I remember in my schooling in one of higher institution of learning. A very learned professor told us that some clever students do not make good grades in their classes because they argue with their professors.

He told us that in the class what is required of you is to listen to your professor and when he presents questions it is not the students' duty to argue or challenge. This is a sign of pride showing that the students know more than him or her.

But he said that once the student has made the grade by giving the answers according to what the professor had taught him: then, after graduation the student can write a book or a magazine article challenging what the professor taught. He has no choice but to listen to what you have to say and it could be that you will help him see the light and accept the criticism.

Living with biases is causing the world to backslide. People not using the knowledge God has given them to check for themselves what others has said. "Politically correct adage" is used to serve this purpose. People need to make their own decisions without the influence from their culture, religion, or other agents.

I regret for the many years I have wasted by following some ideas or doctrines which have been half-truths. I did not think majority could sincerely follow some misleading teaching without discovering they are false or half-truths. But I praise the Lord that he has helped me to see the truth and I have made sure that the truth I have come to know is from the Truth Himself.

I have taken the time to explain this because many people are missing the true knowledge which could liberate them from the bondage of Satan and other people. The Bible says, "My people are destroyed for lack of knowledge." (Hosea 4:6)

For our lives to succeed we need to put first things first. The Bible says that we are "to seek first the kingdom of God and then all these things will be added unto us." (Matt. 6:33). It is true that we do not heed what the Word of God says. Instead, we seek other things first and then the kingdom of God later. In other words, God is not first in our lives and that is why we miss his guidance, blessings and His protection

It is not possible to live a victorious marriage life if God is not put first. We seem to know this already but we do what we want anyway - without God. How can we fail to follow the blue print of our maker who created the marriage institution as our union with one another and with God?

For example, if I look back over my life I have really enjoyed my marriage life so much, yet not as much God had intended. Sometimes I have fallen short of His grace because of pride and foolishness. I have also failed because of my selfishness, failing to fulfill my role satisfactorily.

God had a purpose in having partnership with him. It so that we human can have closer fellowship with him following his command on what he has ordained. There are five important things in marriage: our attention and commitment; service to one another; and daily fellowship with one another and communion with God.

It is these small things which make marriage wonderful. When we look back we are able to discover what has hindered us from enjoying our marriages to the full.

Just to do our part or doing our part as a duty not as a service to God and fellow partner flowing out of love relationship.

We need to adapt God's methods of overcoming evil by doing better and never to seek revenge because revenge and recompense belong to God. We should learn how to deal with our partner's weaknesses by not criticizing them but compete in well going without telling them.

In the book you will discover the hidden wisdom of the summary of the whole book in the sub-topics which are arranged alphabetically from A-Z with some taking more in one alphabet.

In these sub-topics there is all the information you need to know about marriage in summary. In actual fact they are entwined so that they share the same message in a different level or aspect.

These are divided into eight parts which stand like subjects. Please check them on the contents. At the end of each chapter it will end with these words. **Try not to avoid answering my two intriguing questions: "Has God been consulted? Will God be consulted?"**

CHAPTER ONE

Avoid Being Judgmental

"Do not judge lest you be judged. For in the same way you judge, you will be judged; and by your standard of measure, it will be measured to you. And why do you look at the speck that is in your brother's eye, but do not notice the log that is in your own eye? Or how can you say to your brother, 'let me take the speck out of your eye,' and behold, the log is in your own eye? You hypocrite, first take the log out of your own eye, and then you will see clearly to take the speck out of your brother's eye." (Matt. 7:1-5)

The opening word 'avoid' in this book after introduction is a catch word to sensitize you to examine in detail what you are going to read in the book.

In this moment of trying to check what might have happened in your marriage one of the many issues which make marriage life become unbearable is the **critical spirit**. A person becomes judgmental or critical of another sometimes rightly or unjustly. Whatever the case judging or criticizing one another is a weakness. The couple should find a way or correcting some wrongs without being judgmental or critical. To me this has been the most difficult thing to do in marriage. **When critical spirit is avoided the couples can live their marriage without quarreling**.

Be a Person of Fewer Words and More Actions

Let us take seriously the admonition of the Word of God in Proverbs 18:21 which says; "Death and life are in the power of the tongue, and those who love it will eat its fruit." Do you know that this statement has double-edge meaning? On one hand it talks of life if we use words of life. On the other hand it talks of death if we use words of death.

The Word of God is life and the word of Satan is death. If you say what Satan says you will get death sentence. For example, if you say that you have a certain disease or sickness and that you are going to die you will surely die.

In the same way if you say what God says that by Jesus stripes you are healed you will get life. It is so simple.

Isaiah tells us to decide what report are we going to accept or believe?

What happens when doctor tells you that you are going to die? Without arguing with him: do you ask what God says about that disease or situation? It is what you will determine the end result. People who use few words avoid a lot of problems because they don't want Satan know what they are thinking.

They know that Satan put a lot of pressure in our lives so that we will say what we are feeling or what we are thinking and once he knows that he is able to add more pressure until you accept defeat and die. **Do you know that you can refuse** to die? These days I am teaching that God did not change the life span of the human beings – it is 120 years.

The reference of 70 to 80 years was suggested by David when he was comparing the wickedness of the Israel at that particular time. And as preachers are quick to interpret the Bible they missed this as they have misinterpreted many other passages from the Bible.

I cannot deal with this topic in this book but it was a revelation which caught me and I could not fail to write it.

Be careful not to equate a person of fewer words with those fools who have a closed mind: or a person who is naïve or mediocre or shy. **A person with fewer is a person who is wise and speaks his mind with clarity.**

It so surprising that the world has few people who excel in being persons of fewer words more actions. As I thought about this I came to discover that the world is full o people who talk much and do nothing. On the other hand, the good thing does not need advertisement it will sell by its quality. However what is of poor quality needs much publicity to persuade or to manipulate people to like or buy them.

The commercial enterprise has gone overboard in presenting that anything, even that which is worthless, is given value simply because of commercial advertisements. The advertisement game has become the standard rule for every thing. How many people who have been deceived by these adverts? The standards of valuable things or people have been compromised.

That is why it is not easier to be recognized if you are a person of fewer words. This advertisement propaganda has also affected the Church. We see it the way the preachers are introduced. If you are ordinary person and not highly educated you may not be invited to preach because you are thought not to possess quality for accolade.

These Christians go astray when they start bragging about themselves. Telling other that they are saved filled with the Holy Spirit and that they speak in tongues. At the end of their bragging they ask, "What about you?" If you don't have the courage to tell them what they want to hear, they regard you as inferior to them. They humiliate you. Jesus never bragged about himself that he was the Son of God although that is what He was.

"So also the tongue is a small part of body, and yet it boasts of great things. Behold, how great a forest is set aflame by such small fire! And the tongue is a fire, the very world of iniquity; the tongue is set among our members as that which defiles the entire body, and sets on fire the course of our life, and is set on fire by hell.

Who among you is wise and understanding? Let him show by his good behavior his deeds in the gentleness of wisdom." (James 3:5-6, 13) This is the place for a person of fewer words.

Be sure that you know what messes your Marriage

While I will try to put down the list of the things which can mess up people's marriages, I would also like you to take an inventory of what you have discovered as the reason or reasons your marriage was or has not been a happy one.

One very important thing to do more than any other thing is to keep reminding yourself of the danger of forgetting those listed problems: Because if you don't bring those defects or failures into remembrance you will have wasted your time.

The small topics or headings in this book give you the areas which you need to take time to peruse them thoroughly together with your personal findings which are not included in this book. **I always insist that reading and understanding the issues or problems is not enough what is very important is to take what you find and put it into practice.**

James has this to say to us, "But prove yourselves as doers of the word, and not merely hearers who delude themselves. For anyone is a hearer of the word and not a doer, he is like a man who looks at his natural face in a mirror; for once he has looked at himself and gone away, he has immediately forgotten what kind of person he was. But one who looks intently at the perfect law, the law of liberty, and abides by it, not having become a forgetful hearer but an effectual doer, this man shall be blessed in what he does." (James 1:22-25)

Culture norms messes your Marriage

We come from many different cultures and each culture has some important norms which has molded our lives in many ways which control us. If you are of different culture or tribe from your partner you need to check out the difference.

These cultural issues can hold someone so deep and there people who don't ever divorce themselves from their culture. Also there are some religious denominations which have some doctrines which tend to conflict the beliefs of some people. I encourage people to create their own rules to help them to develop their own culture. **Try not to avoid answering my two intriguing questions: "Has God been consulted? Will God be consulted?"**

CHAPTER TWO

Did I really become a Servant?

There is honor and greatness in serving. The leading example is that of the Son of God who came to serve the human beings he created. "For even the Son of Man did not come to be served, but to serve, and to give His life a ransom for many." (Mark 10:45)

I have discovered that many people are interested in marriage because they anticipate the benefit of being served. This is so much with men who many times regard their wives as servants. On the other hand today women marry men of means hoping to get service because of the position of the husband or because of his money.

I feel privileged to have known that I was marrying my wife to serve her. Even up to forty-fives years together I have never failed to serve my wife and I hope this is one factor which has contributed to the happy marriage we have enjoyed so far.

This is why I would like to ask you to reflect on your performance in your marriage and see whether you have neglected this virtue of being a servant. The other element involved in this is self esteem. If you know who you are you will have no problem to serve your partner.

If you have low esteem you will always want to be uplifted by being served. If you have not been a servant in your marriage I would appeal to you to start to day and experience the miracle of transforming your marriage. I remind you again that if Jesus the Son of God came to serve; can't you do the same and take your pride to the cross.

"But not so with you, but let him who is the greatest among you become as the youngest, and the leader as the servant." (Luke 22:26)

Did I take things for granted?

I want you to know what I am doing in this book in every aspect of the subject I am addressing I am requesting you to look back and see how you have done, and then look forward and decide what you are going to do differently.

These days we have a big problem because many people are not serious about their commitments, any thing they take for granted: and therefore they do not succeed in whatever they undertake to do. This is so crucial when it happens in marriage.

In marriage love, forgiveness, commitment, sacrifice, faithfulness, service and upholding the marriage vows are the most important things. These things cannot be taken for granted. I would advice you to take your inventory about how you do these things and how you intend to strengthen them to be the pillars in your marriage.

The fact that marriage is a union and a covenant between two persons and God is supposed to be taken very serious. But I do not think that many marriages have this basic foundation in their minds.

Do not take your baggage in your Marriage

I normally insist always that people should form habits which help them to maintain balance in life. The main thing here starts with the person knowing who he or she is. Every person is supposed to check what he carries in his life by understanding that there are three parts namely: spirit, soul and body.

In each person these three parts have a part to play in influencing the life of a person. But when the spirit takes control, it influences the soul which also influences the body and the outcome becomes the behavior of that person. If the person is not saved, his spirit is dead and easily takes orders from Satan who always does wicked deeds which oppose what God has commanded.

The Bibles talk much about people who are dead in sin and in trespasses (1 Tim. 5:6) People living in pleasure are dead while they are alive.

When the Holy Spirit takes over from the dead spirit of a person he gives life. And the Bible put it very clearly that, "And you hath he quickened, who were dead in trespasses and sins." (Col. 2:1) Explaining what happened, "Wherein in time past ye walked according to the course of this world, according to the prince of the power of the air, the spirit that now works in the children of disobedience:

Among whom also we all had our conversation in times past in the lusts of our flesh, fulfilling the desires of the flesh and of the mind: and we were by nature the children of wrath, even as others. But God, who is rich in mercy, for his great love wherewith he loved us, even when we were dead in sins, hath quickened us with Christ, by grace ye are saved. (Eph. 2:2-5)

I am trying to show that when a person is saved his spirit is revived and made alive. Then through the Word of God the Holy Spirit influences the soul. In the soul realm are mind/intellect, will and emotions.

Enjoy yourself and at the same time enjoy your Partner

There is a saying that if you do good deed to others you are doing it to yourself. This again goes with what the Word of God says, "For whatever a man sows this he will also reap." (Gal. 6:7) Again, "Therefore, however you want people to treat you, so treat them, for this is the Law and the Prophets." (Matt.7:12)

There is always joy when you voluntarily decide to please others. God wanted us to enjoy life by pleasing our partners. To do this we need to uphold discipline to keep us focused so that we don't demand our own ways. Discipline will help us to guard our thought life which will help us determine our right attitudes.

The enemies of this virtue are pride and selfishness which demand service from others instead of giving them service. We shall never be able to give Jesus service enough because He gave himself completely for us.

Functional Marriage tips

Our God is faithful and from him we can learn how to be faithful. Faithfulness is one of God's communicable attributes which we can share with him. He allows us enter into a relationship with him that will make us trust Him completely. But before that time we have to be free from sin and quilt. The truth is that God chose us while we were yet sinners. "But God commends his love toward us, in that, while we were yet sinners, Christ died for us." (Romans 5:8)

God is telling us to, "Stand fast therefore in the liberty wherewith Christ has made us free, and be not entangled again with the yoke of bondage." (Galatians 5:1) The word liberty stands for the word freedom. That means that once we are saved we are free from fear and other bondage of other vices. And it is this freedom which gives us complete faithfulness.

I am really surprised by the way people are behaving these days. Most people are behaving like children. They don't know right from wrong. The leaders and their followers are the same. It is as if homes are run by children who do not know the meaning of building a home where peace and tranquility prevail. When you take a look at the political leadership the picture is the same. When you look at the Church the picture is the same.

Faithfulness in marriage is very important because it allows husband and wife to be free and open with one another. From this freedom of not fearing that you are going to be ignored or accused of being unfaithful help trust to flourish a home. Because of our own weaknesses we are made to think our spouses are the same with us. We portray what is in us as what is in them fueling to maintain the spirit of mistrust.

But when we are confronted by these confusing situations, where can we turn? We are luck that God has not yet closed the door for us to go to him for advice and help. His first advice is from Psalm 127:1-3; Jer. 29:11-13; 33:3; Isa.65:24; Matt. 6:33; 1 John 5:14-15; **Try not to avoid answering my two intriguing questions: "Has God been consulted? Will God be consulted?"**

CHAPTER THREE

God's Factor

This God factor in marriage is the pillar of marriage life. God has to be given his place in marriage. He is to be given a throne in home as well as in the marriage. He should be allowed to lead, guide, protect and provide the daily necessities. As we put God in our heart and mind he will help us to face the daily struggles of life to be able to control what comes to destroy our lives.

To be able to succeed we have to take into account how we react in combating those forces. For example when death takes one of us: when we are fired from work: when we are mistreated and so on. Our reactions will depend on where we get the power to defeat those forces which invade our territories.

But it will be different when we know that, "Greater is He who is in us than he who is in the world." (1John 4:4) We are able to follow the example of those servants of God who have gone before us and do what they did to face those threatening situations.

Daniel when they conspired to throw him in the den of lions. (Daniel 6:10-26) Again how Shadrach, Meshach and Abednego responded when they were faced with death if they did not fall down to worship the image of the gold. But they did not succumb to that threat for they knew that Greater is He who was with them. They faced the fire headlong and overcame.

Our God is not an idea, He is a real person who was, and is, and He is to come. In other words: Jesus is the same yesterday to day and forever. (Hebrews 13:8) "For this is our God for ever and ever; he will be our guide even to the end." (Ps. 48:14)

The God factor brings to us the gift of righteousness which gives us the right standing before God. By this we know that we are justified; we are sinless: we are perfect before God and therefore we don't allow the spirit of feeling unworthy or the spirit of sin's consciousness to deny our position with our God.

We have been given power to live perfect lives in the eyes of God because of what has been done through Jesus Christ. The goodness with this attitude we do not get discouraged when we fail. We can tell the devil and his agents that God has already provided for our escape by our covering with God's righteousness. Thus, whatever devil brings to us we shall see it, feel it but will not make us afraid.

In fact every one who marries should pray that God will give him the partner that is to be his helpmate. And God is faithful and He will do his part. You also have to keep your part which is to enforce the vow which you say in front of God, His servant, your parents and your friends. This is not to be regarded as a common or a joke: it is not a small thing: it is a blessing from God. A good husband or wife is a gift from God.

We have a very vivid God's picture of a woman 'wife' of a noble character, Which is God's picture of what should be.

Proverbs 31:10-31

10 A wife of noble character who can find? She is worth far
more than rubies.
11 Her husband has full confidence in her and lacks nothing
of value.
12 She brings him good, not harm, all the days of her life.
13 She selects wool and flax and works with eager hands.
14 She is like the merchant ships, bringing her food from
afar.
15 She gets up while it is still night; she provides food for
her family
and portions for her female servants. 16 She considers a
field and buys it;
out of her earnings she plants a vineyard. 17 She sets
about her work vigorously;
her arms are strong for her tasks. 18 She sees that her
trading is profitable,
and her lamp does not go out at night. 19 In her hand she
holds the distaff
and grasps the spindle with her fingers. 20 She opens her
arms to the poor
and extends her hands to the needy. 21 When it snows, she
has no fear for her household; for all of them are clothed in
scarlet. 22 She makes coverings for her bed; she is clothed
in fine linen and purple. 23 Her husband is respected at the
city gate, where he takes his seat among the elders of the
land. 24 She makes linen garments and sells them, and
supplies the merchants with sashes.
25 She is clothed with strength and dignity; she can laugh at
the days to come.
26 She speaks with wisdom, and faithful instruction is on

her tongue.
[27] She watches over the affairs of her household and does
not eat the bread of idleness. [28] Her children arise and call
her blessed; her husband also, and he praises her: [29] "Many
women do noble things, but you surpass them all."
[30] Charm is deceptive, and beauty is fleeting; but a woman
who fears the LORD is to be praised. [31] Honor her for all
that her hands have done, and let her works bring her praise
at the city gate.

There has been a lot of misunderstanding about the place of a woman in life and in marriage. The Patriarchal system teachings and influences put a woman as second hand person or a person equal to a slave who is there to serve man and do his bidding.

This is the same system which also introduced slavery and put it in place. I wonder how for a long time people have never discovered the plan of God. For the true plan of God for a woman and her place in marriage is fully displayed in Proverbs 31:10-31 as quoted earlier.

In this plan and picture she is the real helper. God in creation found that the man was helpless and provided the man his helpmate. Also in Ephesians 5:21-32 the Word of God talks of a woman representing the Church and the man representing Christ. And this is the only context where words like love and submit fit perfectly well.

On the contrary, this submission is not an order from man to his wife. This does not make the man to force his wife to submit to him but it is God's order for the man to love his wife as Christ loves his Church and out of that love the wife graciously submit to her husband.

What God allowed the man to be is to shower his wife with love and through this love the wife will be everything a man will ever desire in life. This is the picture according to God's plan. Anything more or less than this is not from God.

Marriage life these days do not fit this pattern and therefore when we are talking about marriage and their modern failures, we are talking a new or created idea of marriage by human beings. Each person has to decide whether he or she goes by the plan of the people or the plan of God. **Your marriage will fail or succeed by your understanding this distinction. Always consider God's factor.**

I don't know why God is left out of the marriage? This is so true for Christians as well as non-Christians. What I think is that those who don't care about life and those who are pagans live their lives without God. To them they have many gods of their own making. Some have taken money to be their god. Others have taken pleasures to be their god: and others have different idols which control their lives. You borrow or create an idea and allow it to control you. Is this not madness?

What I don't understand is how could a Christian who knows that there is one true God can bow to worship these other gods? The main difference is the message of the gospel. The problems which are now in the world are the result of these many gospels. People have come up with many gospels these days. But to me there is only one true gospel: the Gospel of Jesus Christ. This is the Gospel which comes to people with power to change them and the world.

It is this power of the Gospel which transforms the lives of people to live happy and peaceful lives. This is the Gospel which makes married people to stick together through hard times. It is this life lived with God in the center which helps to equip people with power to overcome their shortcomings.

In this world we expect to meet with many hardships and problems and for a person to succeed he needs God. Jesus gave the model for the marriage relationship to imitate the relationship between Christ and his Church. This is where love and submission are equally balanced. These two issues of love and submission have brought so much confusion that has made marriage to loose value. God should be the authority to give orders.

One hidden thing for those who are anticipating getting married is that they never thought that the one of the most important virtue in marriage is **the spirit of servant-hood**. Whenever people are thinking of getting married they thinking of the benefit they will get in marriage. This kind of thinking does not take into account that marriage is the service which those who marry are called to do. And to be able to do it well one has to have **a spirit of a servant.**

We get this picture clearly in two places in the Bible where Jesus is said to have humbled himself in Philippians 2:5-11, "Let this mind be in you, which was also in Christ Jesus: who being in the form of God, thought it not robbery to be equal with God: but made himself of no reputation, and took upon him the form of a servant, and was made in the likeness of men: and being found in fashion as a man, he humbled himself, and became obedient unto death, even the death of the cross.

Wherefore God also hath highly exalted him, and given him a name which is above every name: that at the name Jesus every knee should bow, of things in heaven, and things in the earth, and things under the earth: and that every tongue should confess that Jesus Christ is Lord, to the glory of God the Father."

And in Mark 10:45, "For even the Son of man came not to be served unto, but to serve, and to give his life a ransom for many." I assure you that you will never go wrong any time your motive in service is to serve.

Head knowledge is not enough

Satan tries and succeeds in making you follow your head knowledge and ignore what is valuable and the most important things in life. Make sure that you decide what you hear or listen and what you think and say for this is what makes your life. Always check the source of the information.

Let me take you to rehearsal to test your position. I want to bring the case of Goliath when he appeared to fight the Israelites. The Israelites were so much afraid of Goliath because of his stature, the figure of his body. When David said he would go and fight him he met with the head knowledge you are so small, with no experienced of war.

But David was sure than he was going to defeat and kill the giant.

The words which were spoken by David came from his heart. He spoke his victory before the fight. In fact he won his fight before the fight started. It is true than what you have in your heart is what you have for your success or for your victory.(1 Samuel 17)

Avoid the old story of the serpent and Eve and Adam. The message of this story is to learn how you will avoid the lie and accusations which put the whole world into the mess we are today. It is so surprising that we keep on repeating or re-enacting what happened on the Garden of Eden.

Avoid the playing game of speaking words which do not mean anything words like I am ok while things are collapsing; praising God with the mouth while the heart is far way. They tell people that they are the friends of God when they are more of friends of Satan. (Titus 1:16)

I am so surprised when I see people with the crosses on their necks and bracelets on their wrists and hear what they say and what they do. It makes me wonder what is wrong with them. Do they do that intentionally or they are ignorant of the meaning of the cross and the bracelet with the words 'What Would Jesus Do? Surely, Jesus could not use the dirty words they use and to do what they do is sacrilegious of the high order.

We are more attracted by what we see than what we hear especially we fail to keep the Word of God. This was the case with Eve. As her eyes were fixed on the fruit of the tree of good and evil; she saw that the fruit was good and pleasing to the eyes; and desirable for gaining wisdom: she took and ate! (Gen. 3:6)

This is the old practice which we keep on putting in motion when we are looking for our future life partners. We do not follow the proper way of seeking God's guidance, but follow our own desires. We look with our eyes and what think only what will benefit us. We take the spirit of selfishness into the marriage.

When we have created problems we only speak about the symptoms like Adam. He told God that he hid when he heard the voice of God, because he was naked. (Gen. 3:8) But he was not sorry.

Adam accused Eve, Eve accused Satan to God: they never admitted their fault or sin. The problem which could have been solved once for all has remained to harass human beings ever since. We can easily see the human recipe of telling lies and refusing to accept their sins.

God gave the judgment according to the severity of the offence starting with Satan and to Eve and last to Adam. It was so amazing that I was able to see something I have never see or thought about. I saw for the first time that the authority of the man to rule over woman came as a result of punishment from God. (Gen. 3:16)

While Satan punishment affected him alone and the Eve punishment affected all women: A dam punishment affected the whole creation. He was told that through painful toil he will be able to feed himself. And the name

Eve was given by Adam because she was to become the mother of all living human beings. (Gen. 3:19)

It was not God's will or wish for the human beings to know the knowledge of good and evil because God knew that human beings will mess themselves they way they did. We are witnesses that today the knowledge of good and evil has increased so much that human beings are on a verge of destroying themselves.

From that time of human beings messing up God laid down the salvation plan according to His judgment as shown on Genesis 3:15. God showed his love to us while we were yes sinners God Christ died for us. He crushed the head of Satan. (Rom.5:8)

Another wonderful thing I saw in the creation story is that Eve acknowledged God's help in the business of bringing a human being into the world. (Gen. 4:1) She said, "With the help of the Lord I have brought forth a man."

Highest model for Marriage is the example of Christ and his Church

What a wonderful thing for us to do than following or copying the pattern of our marriage to that model Jesus gives to us. "Submitting yourselves one to another in the fear of God Wives, submit yourselves unto your own husbands, as unto the Lord. For the husband is the head of the wife, even as Christ is the head of the Church: and he is the savior of the body.

Therefore as the Church is subject unto Christ, so let the wives be respectful to their own husbands in every thing.

Husbands love your wives, even as Christ loved the Church, and gave himself for it: That it might sanctify and cleanse it with the washing of water by the word. That he might present it to himself a glorious Church, not having spot, or wrinkle, or any such thing: but that it should be holy and without blemish." (Eph. 5:21-27)

This model contains more than what meet the eyes. It is very particular in every aspect or all details which should be fulfilled to the letter. It deals with the issues of love and submission which are always discussed out of the context. For if the husband does the loving the wife will automatically submit. Just do that and it works.

How can I do things differently?

This is also very important question to ask so as to be able to discover what went wrong. This calls for taking the inventory so that one is aware of the failures which were neglected or were not done. You do this **in the spirit of love and cooperation.**

During this time of examination one need to seek help from experts or help from some books which have those kind of information needed. The book titled "Marriage Without Sex" is the book you should consult.

You will realize that most of what is written in this book is the things you should have learned to do or you should have avoided. When you go through them you will be able to know how you can do things differently if you have not yet known by now. **Try not to avoid answering my two**

intriguing questions: "Has God been consulted? Will God be consulted?"

CHAPTER FOUR

Importance of equal participation in bed

I have counseled many people and one of the problems I encountered is the problem of lack of knowledge about the part each partner should do or play in bed. Many told me that they never thought they needed teaching to know how to behave in bed: **the art of love making**.

There are people who have been married for many years yet the have not mastered that skill. These are the people who behave like animals. In this age and time such performance should be regarded barbaric. It is surprising to know that even those regarded primitive people are more skilled in art of making love.

I would advice you to read my book with the title "Marriage Without Sex' and you will be able to get how you should behave in bed. This is done in a clean way not doing things like the world.

Joyous Marriage

For couples to have a joyous marriage the following factors should be considered. That Jesus Christ is made the head of the home. The couple should learn not to be easily offended. They should value their relationship with God and with one another. Thus, they should allow God to control their hearts minds and mouths.

Many people work hard to show others how they have a happy marriage. But the fact is that it is a just show-off and nothing more. Cultivate marriage happiness in your hearts which sometimes is not openly clear that you have that happiness. Happiness should be your possession and not a borrowed thing. Know who you are and don't pretend what you are not. Work yourself inside out.

It is not true that in a joyous marriage there is peace and happiness all the time. No, but what makes such marriage regarded as joyous is the attitude the couple take in tackling whatever invade their marriage.

They always know that there is an enemy who will try every time to bring chaos in their marriage but they have no place for the enemy to trash his evil thoughts in their lives. They know that they are weak for that reason they don't deal with the enemy they allow the Lord Jesus Christ to do it.

Knowledge is Power.

If you can easily remember all what is written in this small book and be able to put it in your heart and in your thoughts you will discover how important the institution of marriage is. You should know that this was God's idea and He planned it for the happiness of human beings.

With this in mind you should be able to maintain the rules and the regulations which govern the success of marriage. It has been said earlier in different ways and in different words: marriage was made for human survival and human communal existence.

I don't need to repeat that where marriage is respected the atmosphere in that home is peace and prosperity. Who does not need peace of mind; security and prosperity, with joy brought about by unity and fellowship in the home with group of committed to family fabric.

It is true that a home can be heaven on earth but not many people these days are ready to pay the price for such a success. Can you be one of those who can do that? How can you read such a book and fail to regulate your life to much with the information given?

I can feel happy to know that I have helped you and you will also feel happy when you discover that the knowledge is power and has given you power to override your rebellious soul.

Let God receive the glory from your Marriage

God demands that , "Whether, then, you eat or drink or whatever you do, do all to the glory of God (1Cor. 10:31) Again "Whatever you do in word or deed, do all in the name of the Lord Jesus, giving thanks through Him to God the Father." (Col.3:17)

In this life we struggle with evil as Satan tries to influence us to allow him get the glory. Satan knows that if he can prevent the couple to do God's bidding he will be able to destroy the family fabric: and once that is destroyed the pillars for the world justice, peace and prosperity are destroyed.

Therefore, we should note that marriage as the union of husband and wife in heart, body and mind was intended by

God for their mutual happiness for the help and comfort for one another for the glory of God. **In this sense marriage is a covenant between God and husband and his wife.**

As we have talked about the service for one another between the husband and his wife the same service is extended to God to bring glory to His holy name by their faithfulness to God and to one another.

Let us go back to the drawing board.

If we were to marry again how would we do things differently? And because we can not go back and start our marriage all over again, we can improve the marriage we have to be renewed and transformed by what have discovered were the things which messed our marriage.

How do we come to that conclusion? We will have to take stock or inventory to be able to know what went wrong. We shall start from beginning discussing all what we can remember about our success and our failures.

For our success we shall thank God for all those good qualities of life we enjoy with one another and promise to continue doing the same or doing better. For our failures we have to note them and seriously come up with ways and means to stop or eradicate them from our marriage.

Sometimes not many couples who can do that by themselves but those who are not able to do it can invite their closest friends and four of them go through all those weaknesses and help one another to turn a new leaf or page. Those who have no close friends they can trust, they can call their pastor and his wife to come and share the moment with them.

And if that is not possible they can look for a counselor and his partner who would play that part. I know it is not easy and many people have no will to do this. But it must be done so as to start new life in their marriage.

In my second book ‘Marriage Discussions Insights’ I encourage couples to form a daily habit of talking and discussing things in their life. I came up with that book because I had discovered that there many married people who do not have that habit of talking casually. They only talk when they are in mood or they need help or when they are protesting or giving orders.

Other times the husband and wife do not talk to one another but they talk with children and visitors when they visit them. Some are good talkers when they have visitors, but immediately visitors are gone they go back to their mode of keeping quiet.

I advise people to form a habit of talking for fun and even telling stories and some involving children to join their jokes. Do something which can be remembered for a long time. I remembered an incident where my children up to today remind me how I laughed and made everyone to laugh until we though that we were sick. **Try not to avoid answering my two intriguing questions: “Has God been consulted? Will God be consulted?”**

CHAPTER FIVE

Maintain a clean heart and clean mind

The word of God gives us the guidance in this area of maintaining a clean heart and clean mind. Proverbs 4:23; "Watch over your heart with all diligence, for from it flows the springs of life." And in Matthew 12:35; "The good man out of his good treasure brings forth what is good; and the evil man out of his evil treasure brings forth what is evil."

Also Proverbs 16: 1 says, "The plans of the heart belongs to man, but the answer of the tongue is from the Lord." Again Proverbs 16:9; "The mind of man plans his way, but the Lord directs his steps."

We are seeing a pattern here that God plays a big and important role in marriage when he is invited. For your marriage to succeed invite God and make Him your protector and guide of your marriage.

Make rules for yourself

The most important word which helps to mold life is discipline. Learn to discipline yourself that you have no problem accepting discipline. You need to get the Word of God to set the standard. "This book of the law shall not depart out of thy mouth; but thou shall meditate therein day and night, that thou mayest observe to do according to that is written therein: for then thou shall make thy way prosperous, and then thou shall have success." (Joshua 1:8)

You need a standard to follow. You can not depend on peoples' opinions or solely on your own conscience. You need the Word of God. You will need discretion to guard you from making bad decisions. (Pro. 2:11) Habits like drinking, smoking, overeating can lead to an early death. We see that in Proverbs 5:23 that a lack of 'discipline' can kill before time.

God commands that we discipline our children. It is impossible to discipline correctly if we are not disciplined ourselves. They need to be taught by our examples. This is the area where parents extend God's blessings or curses to their children. As the parent upholds discipline and pass it to the children: God will instruct them and teach them in the way which they will follow. (Pro.32:8)

No competition in marriage but you are called to excel in well doing

In my second book '**Marriage Without Sex**' I have emphasized that the couple should always '**compete with each other in well doing**': and this should be the norm. Competition is always for the opposing teams or partners and therefore is anathema in marriage. Again the issue of preferring the other person more than yourself comes in place automatically.

Again the idea of making the two person one flesh is clearly maintained in this attitude of doing things together in unity. The enemy should never be allowed to come in between to separate the couple. Don't allow yourself to be used by the friends or enemies to be the destroyer of your marriage. **Each successful marriage is sustained by giving service wholeheartedly to one another.**

Only you can make your marriage heaven on earth

There is a saying that when you are pointing your finger to the other person you point with one finger but the other three fingers are pointing at you and the thumb point to heaven to declare the verdict. Such symbolism tells a lot of truth. The Bible says don't judge so that you may not be judged. (Matt. 7:1)

Also, "Therefore all things whatsoever you would that men should do to you, do even so to them: for this is the law and the prophets." (Matt. 7:12) **It is therefore, your thoughts, attitudes, words and actions which make your marriage heaven or hell.**

Of late I have come to understand the problem many people face in trying to operate their lives or their marriages. Not many people who take into consideration the fact that a human being is a tripartite being. He has the spirit, soul and body. The spirit is like the palace of the king. The soul is like a parliament and the seat making laws and implementing them. The body is like working class which is used by the spirit (king) and the soul (the ruling class).

The first part of the human being is occupied by spirit. When a person is saved the Holy Spirit comes to occupy the throne. Where the person is not saved or born again Satan occupies the throne. From that vantage either The Holy Spirit or the Evil spirit works downward to influence the soul and body.

The second part of the human being is occupied by the soul. The soul consists of the mind/intellect, the will and the emotion. The soul can be used by the spirit or by the body because it has the operational force to bring things to come to pass. The soul lives for ever it will be the vehicle of sustain the evil spirit in hell.

The body occupies the area of senses. It is also the tent which houses the soul and the spirit. Seeing, hearing, feeling, touching and smelling are the forces body uses to satisfy its appetite.

When Satan has taken over the spirit of a person he is able to control the human life and direct it the way he wants. For example when Satan cheated Eve the he was able to occupy the place which was left vacuum when the Spirit of God left. And because the Spirit of God has life as soon as that life was withdrawn the spirit of the human being died.

This is spoken in many places in the Bible referring when the human race was dead in sins and transgressions. (Eph. 2:1-5; Col. 2:13-20; Rom 5:15; 6:6-15;

One can see now clearly why Jesus died to conquer death so those who believe in him should not die.

The point I want to put across is how people identify themselves. Some identify with the Spirit of God and their lives testify about that. Others identify with the soul or with body that they are carnal or they are dominated by the flesh.

The confusion comes when a saved person has accept or identify with the soul or with the body and wonder what the

Bible talk about their position in Christ is not evident in their lives and wonder why? The reason is when the Holy Spirit took over his life, the other parts; soul and body have to be made to submit to the guidance or leadership of the Holy Spirit. This is brought about through the Word of God which brings the renewal of the mind and transformation of the heart. "For the Word of God is quick, and powerful, and sharper than any two-edged sword, piercing even to the dividing asunder of soul, and spirit, and of the joints and marrow, and is a discerner of the thoughts and intents of the heart." (Heb. 4:12)

In a nutshell one needs to be made with enablement of Go's power to live heaven on earth.

Overcome evil with good

If the married people can start their marriage with this focus of overcoming evil with good they will discover the magic of improving their marriage instead of destroying them. I called this to excel in well doing in my second book, **'Marriage Without Sex**' and it heals a lot of problems in marriage. This is very simple. When your partner does something ugly, instead of complaining you just do the opposite. You reward him by doing something good. This is an indirect teaching or learning.

You excel in well doing.

In every teaching I make I always try to introduce the weapons to be used in the combat zone. If you read all my books starting from **'Marriage Without Sex'** you will discover I emphasize guarding the heart, thoughts and mouth. For any thing which will come to destroy your marriage or your life will involve these three parts.

The Bible gives us the guidance: “Do not be overcome by evil, but overcome evil with good.” (Rom. 12:21) This is the last verse of Chapter 12 of book of Romans and it gives the practical aspect on how to behave to be able to overcome evil with good. **Try not to avoid my two intriguing questions: “Has God been consulted? Will God be consulted?”**

CHAPTER SIX

Personal traits

There are many ways to go round the mountain. In the same ways there are many ways to go about what can help a person to do well in their marriages. We may use different terminologies but these terminologies help some people to understand at their level about the subject addressed.

This is very clearly seen how many people write books which are dealing with the same topic or subject but when you read them you will find the ways the authors apply some phraseologies or vocabularies which they hope will reach their main audiences.

When we deal with personal traits we are anticipating those who have studied psychology will easily understand the method used to explain some marital issues. In other areas these traits are very common words we use in every day language to explain what happens in people's lives.

I have very much tried to avoid such a treatment in this book. In fact most of my books I try to write very simple language which every person can understand.

In the Bible most of the failures or mistakes which people do are called sins. As I have mentioned earlier that some other fields and disciples have their own ways of calling these weaknesses or sins. Whatever the case I try to help people know there are many ways of getting the information one need to know. But always simple messages or information are meant for the people who don't have problems in understanding the meaning of the words used or the language used. But you will not go wrong if you can use the Word of God to check what it says about the problems with the human beings

Promote marriage happiness

This could be a good starting point of two persons agreeing to work hard to promote marriage happiness in their home. Many things do not succeed because the persons involved are not resolved to make their marriage happy. These are the people who know very well that there is an enemy who works overtime to make sure that marriages do not succeed.

To them the devil is their enemy number one who is not allowed to mess about with those who know that they are children of God and that devil was defeated on calvary. What he uses are his old lies that God is not faithful. He told Eve that God was holding back some fruit which could benefit them. We know the result. These days he tells us that we are going to die while he deceived Eve that if she ate the fruit she will never die.

The victory many people don't know how to defeat Satan is by enforcing the calvary victory. Remind him what happened and once you know that secret you will understand the power of the cross. And if there is one thing devil fears is to be reminded what Jesus did.

The mention of the name of Jesus is powerful when you tell the devil that you are standing against him in the name of

Jesus. It is only given for us to call when needing healing or salvation. **"Neither is there salvation in any other: for there is none other name under heaven given among men, whereby we must be saved." (Acts 4:12)**

It is also the name for all to confess. "Wherefore God also has highly exalted him, and given him a name which is above every name: That at the name of Jesus every knee should bow , of things in heaven and things in earth, and things under the earth: and that every tongue should confess that Jesus is Lord, to the glory of God the Father." (Phil. 2:9-11)

Quarrel free marriage

This is a polite way of saying that hygiene is a paramount in marriage. It is rude to tell your partner that he or she is dirty. But when we start discussing about cleanness in marriage we mention about the maintenance of heart and mind. This will not be offensive and will take message home. While we are in this topic we should mention about the use of dirty language which should be a taboo in marriage.

It is true that being dirty, untidiness, careless are signs that your upstairs has some defects or problems. I am talking these days of the problems which are with the human race saying that many people do not know how they come about and how to overcome them.

I am thinking that if people were exposed to the fact that a human being is a tripartite being they will be able, know where to go for help. I have mentioned this teaching somewhere else in this book only in passing because this is not the forum or scope to be able to tackle such a heavy staff: but is a subject one need to know.

In human make up you have spirit, soul and body and each one of these has its own influence to the other two parts. But there is always the confusion in understanding which is the right functional way to allow a human being enjoy life. In a nutshell is when the Holy Spirit takes control of the spirit part and then influences the soul and body to function on its terms. This is why allowing the Word of God to examine your lives will help you avoid taking the poison in your soul or body.

"The Word of God is quick, and powerful, and sharper than any two-edged sword, piercing even to the dividing asunder of soul and spirit, and of the joints and marrow, and is a discerner of the thoughts and intents of the heart." (Heb. 4:12)

Many people do not know the work of the Word of God and how it operates in revealing the hidden evils in ones life. Reading the Word of God it will protect you and your family if you obey.

Resourceful persons

This is one area which has not been taken into consideration in life because not many people who think that they need to make themselves resourceful persons. People need to know that it is their duties each person to learn to equip himself with the information which one will need to use in his life and in his marriage.

I am not talking about going to school as such, but I am sensitizing people to have open mind to learn what goes round in their surroundings. For example, when you are walking, when you are in your working area, when you are watching TV, wherever you are is a ground for your learning.

In your learning journey you are seeing or hearing things which are good for you or things which are detrimental for you. You start very early getting informed what you will face in your whole life and if you are keen to sieving the information you will discover that at a certain level of your learning you have equipped yourself with what is needed to be a resourceful person for marriage and any other area of life.

Take marriage for example. You start gathering information on marriage. You keep your eyes and ears open to see and hear what people do and say by the time you get married you will have gotten all what is needed in marriage. In this personal learning never take things for granted. If you don't understand what you are supposed to do ask and you will be in the position of knowing.

We have internet which is also a source of information: use it for your learning. To days things which took time to get or to know they are there at your nose.

Secret of two persons becoming one flesh

Another hidden thing from human being is what happens when two persons a man and a woman become one flesh. This is different from the animal kingdom. And it was for this reason sex was forbidden for those who are not married because it was a custom to prepare them to that sacred moment of becoming one flesh. Because of sin people did rebel from heeding God's commandments and therefore the problems which we experience up to today.

It is very clear that premarital or extramarital sex producing people in the world who have no manners or norms to follow. That is why we have a generation which has made world as the world lived by brutes. Generation which behave like animals and it does not matter whether these people are educated or not. It is such a pity.

Take order from God

The most secure and direct way to do things is to make God your first priority. That means that you will not do any thing without consulting or seeking direction or order from God. In life as well as in marriage there are many decisions to make, and some decisions are very much overwhelming: but because with God all things are possible and that there is nothing too hard for him, you are sure to succeed.

Some couples have found solace in asking God's directions in prayers. They are committed never to buy and thing before they have asked permission from God. This really makes God part of the union in marriage.

In any situation you find yourself in and you are not sure what to do even if you can ask for help from human beings let God be the final deciding factor in all tat you do. "Be careful for nothing; but in every thing by prayer and supplication with thanksgiving let your request be made known unto God." (Phil. 4:6)

God directed Joshua to take order from the book of the law. "This book of the law shall not depart from your mouth, but you shall meditate on it day and night, so that you may be careful to do according to all that is written in it; for then you will make your way prosperous, and then you will have success." (Joshua 1:8) The summary is to get wisdom. "To know wisdom and instruction: to perceive the words of understanding; to receive the instruction of wisdom, justice, and judgment, and equity." **(Pro. 1:2-3) Try not to avoid my two intriguing questions: "Has God been consulted? Will God be consulted?"**

CHAPTER SEVEN

Take your heart, mouth, and mind or thoughts to prison

I am always advocating that the heart, thoughts and mouth should be tamed so as to keep in tune with life of the newly married couples. I have used a different term or approach by saying that you take your heart and thoughts and mouth to prison. Prison is the place where things are done according to the laid down regulations. This becomes clear when you discover that you don't belong to yourself you belong to someone else whom you serve with every part of your being

In Proverbs we can learn many things which we need to do or avoid. "A man shall be satisfied with good by the fruit of his mouth: and the recompense of a man's hands shall be rendered unto him." (Pro. 12:14) Also "He who speaks truth tells what is right, but a false witness, deceit." (Pro. 12:17) This shows that a man's character is revealed by what he says.

On the other hand Proverbs 23:7 says, "For as he thinks within himself, so he is." By now we know what to take to prison. We should never become part of a rumor. We should avoid nagging because it is a bad problem especially with women. "A constant dripping on a day of steady rain and a contentious woman are alike." (Pro. 27:15) But even today men are not spared.

True love is a gift from God and you cannot give what you don't have

These days I allow people to talk about practical love so that you can easily understand what one is talking about. Love as an idea or theory is what many people have: but when love is an abstract it means many things to different people.

You can not give an abstract love because it is not tangible. In the first place love is person. God is love. And love comes from God. The good news is that God gives love freely even to those who don't deserve. "But God commends his love toward us, in that, while we were yet sinners, Christ died for us." (Romans 5:8)

There are many places in the Bible where God has shown or given his love. "For God so loved the world that he gave his only begotten Son, that whosoever believes in him should not perish, but have everlasting life."(John 3:16) In 1 Corinthians 13 which is called the love chapter explains what love does. In verses 4-8, we have the summary of what true love is. I would encourage you to read it by yourself.

Beloved, let us love one another: for love is of God; and every one that loves is born of God, and knows God. He that loves not knows not God; for God is love. (1John 4:7-8)

Uninterrupted marriage honeymoon

There are things which are easier said that done. This is one of them. There are many reasons as to why any couple in the whole world can not practice uninterrupted marriage honeymoon. But I know some couples who try to maintain this idea although there are many things which come to interfere with it.

One thing should be clear that when couple goes for honeymoon, they have few things to do. It is eating, sleeping and resting or walking for leisure. In this area there people who are there to serve. When they come back to their home environment there are many things to attend to. It now becomes a matter of priorities and commitments to fulfill them.

But when this is understood and put in its proper perspectives: the couple will be able to know that they have started putting in practice the things they will live to do for the rest of their lives.

Therefore, honeymoon should continue throughout the whole life of the marriage being used to be as a time to jumpstart and bring to life when love diminishes. Without this marriage becomes a prison or a burden. This is when two separate human beings volunteering to become one flesh for the purpose of cementing their marriage relationship.

Unstable marriage

Do not go very far in your marriage without realizing that unstable marriage is made by unstable people, and you could be one of them. If you don't know how to deal with the wrong which come to us all you will always blame others. The problem could be you, or the other partner or both of you and the solving of such problems need God's help.

There are a lot cries about marriages which have failed. You could be one of those who are living in these marriages. **A failed marriage is the marriage which does not meet the needs which are meant to be met in marriage.**

This book has mentioned many problems which have been allowed to enter into the marriage and as a result these vices have caused the marriage to fail. For you to prevent your marriage not to be categorized on the list of **the failed marriages** you should heed what has been said in this book.

In the first place make sure that you put the first things first. Second you should guard those important factors which are the pillars of a stable or successful marriage. I feel I don't need to keep on hammering these things on you because if you are serious in your daily check your performance there is a guarantee that you will succeed. **The ball is on your court.**

Veracity in marriage

When I talk of veracity in marriage I just try to emphasize the importance of truthfulness in marriage. The main thrash in this is the weight I put on the truth as the cornerstone of marriage.

You can classify marriage into many components but in the real sense the difference is the slight meaning of the word.

Again the differences are brought about by the emphasis some people put on some words on their importance.

You will hear some people say that faithfulness in marriage is very important. Other will come up saying commitment, communication, openness, love, sacrifice and many more. What this means is that the difference is where some people put their emphasis according to their classification.

Violence in marriage

I wonder why don't people pause and try to ask some searching questions which could help them avoid many pitfalls in their marriages. We know that it is only few marriages which are not given proper planning before they take place. And others on this level are those forced or arranged marriages even without the consent of those involved.

For such marriages to fail it is understandable. But again there are very few marriages in this category which end up being successful. What do we make of this? As we have stated earlier that people who are so unselfish and so committed to make their marriages successful are able to turn things round and get good results. This again removes some excuses which make some people blame parents or other people for the failures of their marriage.

Was there a proper foundation?

Again this is a very important question to ask and try to get the needed answers. What I have discovered is that many marriages fail for lack of sound or firm foundation. Many people marry because it is something done by many people all over the world. But as it is imperative for a builder when he start thinking about building a house he would need a plan; after plan prepare the place and the ground for building, and then get the material to the site afterward the building can begin. The same is with marriage. This is a preparation stage.

In actual building the most important thing is the foundation. Firm foundation will make the house firm able to weather the storms which can happen to the house after it is completed. If the foundation is weak that house will bring a lot of problems which at time can make the house uninhabitable. We have an example of Jesus parable on two builders. One built on the rock and the other one on sand and when the rain and the waves hit those two houses: one house fell and the other house stood. (Matt. 7:24:27

My second book **'Marriage Without Sex'** has the two most important helps which any person contemplating to marry need to consider. The first one is preparation and the second is the information needed for making a marriage a success**. Try not to avoid my two intriguing questions: "Has God been consulted? Will God be consulted?"**

CHAPTER EIGHT

Watch for small foxes

In my counseling for many years I have found that what breaks marriage are those small things which are neglected and taken for granted. That is why I have given this heading: **'Watch for small foxes'**. I have known many people who have messed up their marriages and have not discovered these small foxes. These small foxes are foolishness, pride, laziness and carelessness. **Not many people who think that they do foolish things; that they are lazy and careless**.

The problem comes when one partner point one or more of these in ones life, when that happen he or she think that he or she is regarded like a child. But if each one was able to accept the way they behave their good marriage could be saved.

I don't know why people regard themselves as perfect and are not ready to be corrected. No human being is perfect. Trying to pretend to be what you are not will always put you on defense as you try to cover your weaknesses.

Admitting that you are not perfect and that you may need help and correction open the way to discuss issues in marriage with clear and open mind. **If you think that you are perfect you have a closed mind and you need help.**

Xero marriage season

As I have indicated that in my books I try to avoid using big vocabularies unless where is not avoidable: here is that place I have used the word '**xero**' which means dry. As I am going through alphabetical order I could not get another word which could substitute this word.

But once you know that I am talking about the marriage dry season then you will be able understand what I am talking about. Most marriages go through some dry seasons which happen once or more times depending on the reasons which make them happen.

Some of these seasons come about during holidays where unplanned money is spent and at the beginning of the year the couple will experience financial hiccups. This happens so much during Christmas time or at other time winter or summer times when expenses go up.

There are others which happen at a certain time when the bills go up and the money is not forth coming especially at the end of the month. But all in all the couple could take some measures to alleviate or stop those types of dry seasons by reducing their unnecessary expenses. But where that is not possible the couple should be ready to accommodate them.

On the whole, preparedness is the most important thing to do so that things which are possible to averted or stopped are taken into account. **In this case discipline and change of behaviors are called in play.**

You are a child of God and you are growing up leaving the childish things behind.

In every stage of growing we meet with those cases which are supposed to be dealt with at each stage. I wish to mention one stage to serve as an example. The teething stage, which brings some problems to most of children disturb those who do not understand why and what happens during that stage. Some parents get worries thinking that the child has develops a certain disease and even take their children to see the doctors.

You will come across some problems which you were not prepared during your early stage of your marriage: but if you are determined to persist and learn you will out grow the problems and when you look back you will discover that it was your childish attitudes which made you behave the way you behaved. **'Always take note that information is power'.**

I am so much amazed to see how many Christians struggle to live their Christian lives. From when they are born again they are confused by what they see as the world standard and are easily drawn to follow. This can't be. When they were born again they were translated into the kingdom of God which has different rules and standards.

They are easily disappointed when they fail to keep the commandments and they blame themselves for all their shortcomings. This is devil's strategy to keep them in darkness. What they need to know is that they need to grow. I do understand that not many of them receive the teachings they so badly need to grow.

They need discipleship. Jesus did not call us into his kingdom to make converts as we see today that the Church is so busy doing. Seventy-five percent of so called

Christians are not prepared to be disciples, but they remain babies in Christ.

The Church is so busy teaching denominationalism and dividing Christians in small groups who are taught to regard themselves as the only true Christians or Church. No competition is allowed in marriage but you are called to excel in well doing.

Your partner is an angel but the accuser of brethren will tell you that he is a devil.

This is one of the secret every person has to know. We have an enemy who works overtime to make sure than we will never succeed in what we are doing. His name is the devil or Satan. He is the accuser of the brethren. The first thing he will do to you is to whisper to you to tell you or to show you how your partner is bad, how he is not faithful, how he does not mean what he says and many other accusation like that.

Be advised and informed never to listen to him. Tell him that your partner is a true servant of God and God has promised to help him not to accept what you are accusing him of. Therefore whenever you have some misgiving or accusation about your partner take it lightly and seek God's guidance on the matter. Some where else I have mentioned about God being involved in marriage and this is a good time to invite him to give counsel.

Also be informed that there will be those friends or foes those who are going to be used by the devil to come and accuse your partner to you. Take no heed. Tell them that you have not employed them to be checking on your partner. And if that comes from your friend you should know that is not a true friend. A true friend can not do that to a friend. Make sure that your heart has no place for hearsay. Your heart is not a trash pit.

I wonder how people allow themselves to be burden with evil thoughts which make them the source of all tricks and maneuvers from the devil. They are always thinking how to find fault with their partners and with all other people. They are the devil workshop. These are the people you can not please in any way. They are the people who are never satisfied. They are open grave.

While on this topic be careful yourself never to be used by the devil to accuse others. God has not given you that role. "Having a good conscience; that, whereas they speak evil of you, as of evildoers, they may be ashamed that falsely accuse your good conversation in Christ." (1 Pet. 3:16) Proverbs 30:10, "Accuse not a servant unto his master, least he curse thee, and thou be found guilty."**The summary is to hate evil. "The fear of the Lord is to hate evil: pride, and arrogance, and the evil way, and the forward mouth, do I hate." (Pro. 8:13)**

Zealous in marriage

As we have dealt with these points one by one we are aware that we are bombarded with the instructions and suggestions as to how to keep our marriage from breakage. Whatever we say has to have the personal will to do it. Knowing and saying things will not change a thing.

The other day I overheard some people talk saying what they thought would make marriage stable. They starts by saying that the number one factor is to build infidelity-proof strategy: keeping the romantic fire burning, watching for inside and outside predators, and having a routine of working your marriage constantly.

They talked about the problems with in-laws and the problem of bringing up children. But these issues with proper understanding and proper commitment are easily solved. For your information you don't start solving them when they start. The preparedness of what people will meet in marriage is crucial. People should discuss how they are going to deal with these before marriage. **Try not to avoid answering my two intriguing questions: "Has God been consulted? Will God be consulted?"**

CONCLUSION

If you have not mastered the message of this book it can be summed in these few words which have been mentioned nearly in every chapter. The God Factor allows God to be the center of the marriage. **God is the one who planned for the creation of marriage institution and as such he needs to be consulted to be able to help his creatures to know and do what he had anticipated.**

I have done round trip in talking about those attributes and aspects which give marriage as an only institution which can help bring peace in the whole world. If we can have happy families where peace and stabilities are functioning properly the result will be reflected in all those families live.

The sub-topics in this book all deal with the way the marriage institution should function and how to salvage those marriages which are in trouble as well as giving the guidance to that end.

The book does not put doing methods or teachings which are given in seminars and conferences, instead it deals with the inner qualities which will enhance marriage peace and stability.

Although the issue of a human being as a triune being has not been brought very clearly to the fore the author has in his minds that the proper cooperation of these three parts in a human being will endeavor to make marriage peaceful. And that is why he has dealt with the inner issues in human operation of the spirit, soul and body.

That is why I have talked so much about God factor. And because if God is given his rightful place in marriage He will help those in marriage weather the storms of life.

The Bible is the manufacturer manual and for any person in whichever level in his walks of life has to read the Word of God as a road map for life. Joshua 1:8 is a very good place to start and continue daily so that according to what that verse says will be able obey it and then be able to prosper and succeed in life.

In Hebrews 4:12, "For the Word of God is quick, and powerful, and sharper than any two-edged sword, piercing even to the dividing asunder of soul and spirit, and of the joints and marrow, and is a discerner of the thoughts and intents of the heart.'' This verse shows how God operates in human beings lives.

The second thing I would like you to remember about this book is a constant reminder of creator of the universe. Whether you are religious or not, you have no excuse not to consult Him. If you don't know He has all the answers any human being needs now or in the future.

He gives advice that, "My people are destroyed for lack of knowledge." (Hosea 4:6) To avoid destruction which we know has destroyed many people in the past, we need to consult Him. He is no respecter of persons. Every body has an open door to approach Him.

Listen to the following testimony: "The God who made the world and all things in it, since He is Lord of heaven and earth, does not dwell in temples made with hands;

Neither is He served by human hands, as though He needed anything, since He Himself gives to all life and breath and all things; and He made from one, every nation of mankind to live on all the face of the earth, having determined their appointed times, and the boundaries of their habitation.

That they should seek God, if perhaps they might grope for Him and find Him, though He is not far from each one of us; for in Him we live, and move and exist, as even some of your own poets have said, 'For we also are His offspring'.

Being then the offspring of God, we ought not to think that the Divine Nature is like gold or silver or stone, an image formed by the art and thought of man.

Therefore having overlooked the times of ignorance, God is now declaring to men that all everywhere should repent, because He has fixed a day in which He will judge the world in righteousness through a Man whom He has appointed, having furnished proof to all men by raising Him from the dead." (Acts 17:24-31) NASB

THE AUTHOR

The Rev. Dr. Stephen N. Ireri is the president of Torati Vision International; he is a pastor, evangelist, marriage counselor, teacher, administrator and author.

Dr. Ireri writes to the majority of frustrated married couples who have given up on the marriage, relegating its functions to their childhood or irrelevance. He says that if you are one of them, then Marriage Second Chance is for you.

What a dynamite way to draw all those who are intending to get married and also for those who have been married to uphold the marriage institution.